NATIONAL GEOGRAPHIC

Wild PONIES

PIONEEER EDITION

By John Micklos, Jr.

CONTENTS

The July morning is hot. Yet a crowd of people stands in the sunshine. These people do not mind the heat. They are excited. They are about to see wild ponies.

The ponies live on Assateague Island. Once a year, cowboys round them up. They herd the ponies to another island named Chincoteague. How do the ponies get from one island to the other? They swim!

Splash! The ponies swim across a waterway. It is called a **channel.** Their trip takes about five minutes.

The ponies reach Chincoteague. They step out of the water and onto the beach. People cheer. The ponies have arrived!

BY JOHN MICKLOS, JR.

In the Swim.
Wild ponies swim from Assateague Island to Chincoteague Island.

'd PONIES

Assateague Island's Mane Attraction

Salty Snack.
The wild ponies eat a salty plant called cordgrass. Every spring, baby ponies are born on Assateague Island. The young ponies eat cordgrass too.

The Pony Sale

Soon cowboys herd the ponies to town. The next day, the young ponies are sold. Why sell the ponies?

- The pony sale raises money for the local fire department.
- The sale also keeps the number of ponies down. The island can feed only a few ponies.

History and Mystery

Wild ponies have lived on Assateague Island for hundreds of years. How did they get there? No one knows for sure. Most experts think the ponies came from England. People brought them when they moved to America. Later, people turned the animals loose on the island.

JAMES L. STANFIELD/GETTY IMAGES

Book Link

MARK THIESSEN

A Whinny-ing Book

Read *Misty of Chincoteague* by Marguerite Henry (Simon & Schuster). This famous book first appeared in 1947 and has helped children all over the world learn about the ponies.

Small in Size

People call these animals ponies. That is because they are small like ponies. They are less than 58 inches tall. Yet they are actually horses. Why are they so small? Life on the island is hard.

The island is a harsh **habitat,** or home. In the summer, the weather is hot. Insects bite. In the winter, the weather is cold and windy. Life on the island is not easy for ponies.

Pony Groups

The ponies live together in small groups called **bands.** Some bands have only two ponies. Others may have a dozen ponies.

Each band usually has one **stallion.** That is an adult male. His job is to protect the band.

A band also has adult females called **mares.** In spring, the mares have babies. The mares care for the new ponies while they grow.

There are many bands of ponies on the island. Together, they form two groups, or **herds.** One lives on the Maryland side of the island. The other lives on the Virginia side. A fence keeps the herds apart.

MARK WILSON/GETTY IMAGES

Pony Numbers

Assateague is not a big island. It has enough food for only about 300 ponies. Yet mares have new babies each spring. How does the number of ponies stay at the right size?

People control the size of one pony herd with a **vaccine.** It is a kind of medicine. The vaccine keeps mares from having babies that year.

The pony sale controls the size of the other herd. A few of the ponies are sold each year. The sale raises money for the fire department. It also helps the ponies.

The pony sale lets some ponies go to new homes. The rest of the herd returns to the island. They will roam free—and have plenty to eat.

On the Fence.
It is not always easy to choose a favorite pony at the pony sale.

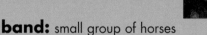

ATLANTICPICTURE/SHUTTERSTOCK.COM

WORDwise

band: small group of horses

channel: waterway between two areas of land that lie close to each other

habitat: place where something lives

herd: large group of horses (often with many bands)

mare: adult female horse

stallion: adult male horse

vaccine: medicine

Pony Parts

The Assateague ponies are small compared to other horses. Yet they have had big success in their island home. What parts help these tough ponies live in the wild?

Eyes
A pony's eyes are on the sides of its head. When a pony is standing still, the only places it can't see are the spots directly in front and behind it.

Tail
Ponies can swing their tails to swat flies and other pesky insects off their bodies.

Hair
In summer, the ponies have thin coats of short, silky hair. In winter, their coats get thick and keep them warm in cold weather.

Legs
Ponies have long legs that let them run quickly away from danger. Long legs are also good for walking through tall grass and bushes.

Hooves
Each hoof has a hard covering. This lets ponies walk or run safely on many surfaces.

Island Refuges

Piping plover

Fly By. Many of the island's birds do not live on the islands. They visit on their way to their winter and summer homes.

Chincoteague and Assateague are famous for their ponies. Yet other animals live there too. The islands are home to many kinds of wildlife.

Parts of each island are protected. That means there are rules about what people can do. In these areas, the wildlife is safe.

Safe Spaces

The Chincoteague National Wildlife Refuge is one of the protected areas. It includes land on both islands.

Many animals live in the refuge. Some live in sand dunes. Others like the marshes, or soggy land. Some make homes in the forest.

Flocking to the Islands

The islands also give shelter to traveling animals. Some birds live in the north during the summer. When the weather turns cold, they fly south. They travel many miles to their warm winter homes. In spring, they fly back along the same path.

All that flying gets tiring. Where do these birds rest? They stop at Chincoteague and Assateague Islands.

Sika deer

Squirrel

Willet

Wet and Wild

Life is pretty wild on the islands. Wind whips the sand from place to place. Water washes the sand away. Yet plants and animals find a way to survive.

Tough grasses grow along the beach. Ghost crabs burrow in the sand. Many kinds of shellfish live in marshes. These are areas where ocean water covers the land.

Life in the Forest

The islands also have forestland. Tall pine trees grow from the sandy soil. The pine trees give food and shelter to many animals.

Squirrels leap from tree to tree. Owls hunt from the treetops. Deer and wild ponies roam the forest floor. They nibble on bushes and plants. Foxes and raccoons also find meals in the forest.

New Horizons. The refuge is a protected area. It helps animals and plants survive.

Safety in the Wild

The refuge does more than protect the land. It helps animals survive.

Bald eagles and piping plovers are in danger of dying out. The refuge gives them a safe habitat. The birds can find food. They have a place to raise their young.

The islands are full of amazing plants and animals. The refuge gives them safe homes in the wild.

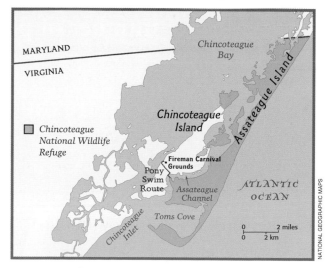

Wet Land. Chincoteague and Assateague are narrow islands. They are between the bay and the Atlantic Ocean.

11

ISLAND LIFE

Take a run at these questions to see what you have learned.

1 Why do ponies swim to Chincoteague Island?

2 Are the ponies on Assateague Island really ponies? Explain.

3 Why is life hard for wild ponies?

4 Why do people control the number of ponies on the islands?

5 Why are the islands good homes?